MINI-S

C000000983

for the Four
Color Personalities

How to Talk to our
Network Marketing Prospects

KEITH & TOM "BIG AL" SCHREITER

Mini-Scripts for the Four Color Personalities
© 2019 by Keith & Tom "Big Al" Schreiter

Published by Fortune Network Publishing
PO Box 890084
Houston, TX 77289 USA

Telephone: +1 (281) 280-9800

BigAlBooks.com

ISBN-10: 1-948197-36-7

ISBN-13: 978-1-948197-36-6

Contents

BIG AL
WORKSHOPS

I travel the world 240+ days each year.
Let me know if you want me to stop in your
area and conduct a live Big Al training.

BigAlSeminars.com

FREE Big Al Training Audios

Magic Words for Prospecting

plus Free eBook and the Big Al Report!

BigAlBooks.com/free

PREFACE

We assume you've already read the book, *The Four Color Personalities for MLM*. In that book we described the four different personalities and how to recognize them.

We also gave examples of the type of language we would use for each color personality to invite them to an opportunity meeting.

This book continues that conversation. We will show examples of how to talk to each color personality in their own native language for many different situations.

Need a "cheat sheet" of phrases to help us communicate better with our prospects? This book will make it easy.

Prospects judge us quickly – within the first few seconds. It isn't fair, but it is the reality. This book will focus on the first words and phrases in our conversations with prospects.

Can we use these short words and phrases in text messages or emails? Of course. But these words are more effective when talking to people in person or over the phone. Now our prospects hear our voice or see our body language. Limiting ourselves to a simple text message removes **us** from the message.

Having a better understanding of the color personalities will enhance our relationships with others. So let's continue the fun of talking to people in a way where they understand our message and bond with us.

When we describe the color personalities in this book, we will be using exaggerated generalizations. This makes them easier to remember. Of course no one's personality is completely one color. But, most people have a dominant color personality. We want to talk to this color personality so they will understand our message.

And finally, many thanks to Yvonne Fausak Kuchta. When two green personalities write about the yellow personality, it is good to have an expert to check the facts.

FLUFFY CAT???

"This is the greatest opportunity in the history of the universe. Our products are unique. No one else has them. The market desperately wants these products. And you can earn $100,000 a year!"

My prospect looked at me and said, "I heard your fluffy cat had kittens last week."

What???

I felt like my prospect was coming from an alternate universe. Something was definitely off-balance, but I couldn't figure out what.

This was my life before I learned the color personalities.

Sound familiar?

Sometimes we talk to people and they don't "get it."

Here I was, talking to a yellow personality, and I had no idea what to do. I was talking, but my message wasn't being heard.

My yellow prospect got up, collected her gemstones, and mounted her unicorn. Then she and her aura of empathy rode off into the rainbow sunset. At least she left me a box of cookies and some angel cards.

Time to learn how to talk to the four different personalities.

How to talk to yellow personalities.

If we are not familiar with the yellow personality, here is a quick overview.

The yellow personalities love to help. They have empathy, think about others first, and find happiness and fulfillment by improving other people's lives. The only word we need to remember to understand their language is "help."

Think of yellow personalities as kindergarten school teachers, grandmothers serving cookies, cheerful customer service representatives, and that school counselor who cared about our future. These examples are a bit much, but they will help us remember that the main motivation of yellow personalities is to help others improve their lives.

Other motivators for yellow personalities? Peace and harmony for themselves and others. They want people to get along and to enjoy their lives. "Happiness for everyone" is their motto. They won't waste their time with emotional outbursts, angry feelings, and grudges. Their comfort zone involves following the rules, supporting the team, and avoiding conflict.

Their biggest asset? Empathy. This helps them connect with all prospects, no matter how difficult they are. Prospects instantly feel that yellow personalities are trustworthy and sincere.

Social situations? Yellow personalities are polite and will wait their turn to talk. This means that sometimes we will never hear from them. They are not antisocial, but find comfort in being alone with quiet time. If yellow personalities are invited to a party (and actually show up), you can usually find them in an adjoining room making friends with the resident pets. Or they will be tucked away in a corner, in deep conversation with someone they feel connected to.

The words.

Words will help us recognize people with yellow personality traits. If we make the effort to listen, these words will stand out. Look for these words in conversations, in messages, and in their social media posts.

Here are some common words used by yellow personalities:

Help.

Advice.

Aid.

Benefit.

Comfort.

Cooperate.

Encourage.

Guide.

Serve.

Service.

Support.

Burden.

Assist.

Hardship.

Cure.

Lift.

Love.

Nourish.

Save.

Cheer.

Stress.

Trouble.

Happy.

Worry.

Meaning.

Connect.

Fulfilled.

When we hear words such as these, we are most likely talking to a yellow personality.

What are the priorities of a yellow personality?

People first, tasks second.

Yellow personalities are relationship-driven. They build the strongest and deepest relationships of the four color personalities. Facts, data, and projects are important, of course. But they are not priorities. Yellow personalities are dependable and competent, but they first consider how their work affects their relationships.

People are their focus. On a deeper level, they take time to consider how other people feel. Yellow personalities ponder, "How will my actions affect others?" And while pondering the effects, they don't feel the need for instant decisions and action. Instead, they may be waiting for inspiration from within. We have to be patient.

"What do other people think? How will other people feel? Am I drawn to this? Does this fulfill my life's purpose?" These thoughts come first in the yellow personalities' minds.

If we focus on relationships when talking to yellow personalities, then we connect. It is not the data or facts that determine our connection. The connection comes from the trust between us.

Do yellow personalities want to know how we feel?

Of course they do.

But they also want to know how we want them to feel. Don't make them guess our intentions.

We can connect quickly with yellow personality prospects by letting them know exactly how we want them to feel about what we offer.

For example, we could say, "Our mission is to help young mothers get better nutrition for their children. This product makes sure that their children get all the basics. I would like you to help me share this option so more mothers know about it. We can make a difference not only in young children's health, but in their ability to learn."

Pretty clear.

People prejudge us, even yellow personalities.

We only have a few seconds to make a good first impression. Let's use these seconds to open the minds of our prospects so they hear our message. Once our message is inside our prospects' heads, they can decide if it will serve them or not.

We don't have to be a salesman. We don't have to push prospects to make a decision. All we have to do is get our message inside our prospects' heads. They are intelligent people. They have common sense. They will know if what we offer will serve them or not.

If we start our conversation with words that resonate with someone's color personality, they hear our message loud and clear.

How much time do we have? Not much. Many times people make their final decision about us when they see our face. Others decide where we will fit into their lives by judging the first sentence out of our mouth.

Yes, we have to be careful about the words we use to start conversations.

When we start our conversations, which words will we use for the yellow personalities?

Yellow personality language examples.

If we talk in the "yellow" language, it is easier for them to understand our intentions. These examples help us focus on their desire for emotional connection.

- "Everything happens for a reason."
- "I want to be sure what I share is meaningful."
- "Does this resonate with you?"
- "If we share with good intentions, we trust our business will grow."
- "How would you feel about sharing these products with others?"
- "How do you feel about getting more natural healthcare options into people's lives?"

It is more about the connection than the message. Messages are good. But for yellow personalities, it is the bonding that makes the difference.

Are yellow personalities all about mystical connections, auras, unicorns, emojis, vibrations, and the position of stars in the universe?

No. But it seems that way to task-oriented personalities such as the red personalities or the green personalities. There is a strong chance of miscommunication. Task-oriented personalities focus on their message. That's why they miss out and don't connect with the yellow personalities.

The yellow personality secret.

Yellow personalities love to bond with the presenter, and then support that person's mission.

Here is a test of our empathy with yellow personalities.

We say, "I want to invite you to our work-at-home conference. It would be great if we could go there together."

Now, what is the motivation of the yellow personality that we are talking with?

A desire to attend the work-at-home conference?

Or, a desire to support us by coming with us?

Yes, yellow personalities will love the family culture of the conference. But their primary motivation is to support us.

Phrases for presenting.

Start our presentations with these phrases to connect to our yellow personality prospects.

- "You can help more people."
- "We need your help."
- "We need to share this."
- "Now our work has meaning."
- "Most people I show this to love how it helps families."
- "Most people I show this to love how it can bring their spouse home."

- "Most people I show this to love how it helps their kids dream."
- "Here is your chance to connect."

We have a lot of choices. Let's see how these phrases would sound in real life.

"You can help more people when you become a distributor with our business. So many people need this product, but they don't know about it. If you could help us share this message, so many people would appreciate what you did for them."

"We need your help so we can reach the elderly community. They want to live longer. They want better health so they have more time with their grandchildren. You can be our voice to share this solution with them."

"We need to share this. Most men would love having the extra income to bring their wives home. Now there would be more quality family time and everyone would be happier."

"Now our work has meaning. Instead of moving paper from one side of a desk to another, we could actually change families' lives. We can have a full-time career while feeling the satisfaction of helping others."

"Most people I show this to love how it can help families. The extra income from our business means more holidays, better holidays, and family memories that last forever."

"Most people I show this to love how it can bring their spouse home. With both parents working from home, they can attend their children's events. Now they can live the dreams they had when they got married."

"Most people I show this to love how it helps their children dream. Their children learn the excitement of having a family business. Now they can dream about the universities they wish to attend, and the lifestyle they want when they graduate."

"Here is your chance to connect with people and help improve their lives. We will feel satisfied from our work, and every day will feel great."

Phrases for selling.

Need a few phrases to say when we are selling our products or services?

- "So many people need this."
- "Here is your chance to help."
- "Now this can help."
- "We need you to share your results."
- "This product/service helps people."
- "This will make a difference."
- "Sharing would help everyone."

Here are examples using these phrases.

"So many people need this discount savings plan. The extra money they save will make a huge difference. Many families struggle every month to make their paycheck go far enough. We can help them make it through the entire month."

"Here is your chance to help people lose their unwanted weight and feel better about themselves."

"Now this can help the elderly. Instead of never having enough energy for the grandchildren, now they can have great life experiences taking their grandchildren to fun places."

"We need you to share your results. Keep copies of your old electricity bill. Then show your friends and family your new, lower electricity bill from us. They will appreciate seeing the proof and feel better about making the change."

"This skincare system helps teenagers get rid of their acne. Teenagers struggle with their self-images. Helping them remove their acne is a huge step forward for them."

"This will make a difference in the lives of young mothers. They can work from their homes, and still be with their families."

"Sharing these natural cleaning products helps everyone. Less pollution and fewer chemicals in our community is our biggest priority."

Phrases to avoid.

Yes, we can offend the yellow personalities also. Yellow personalities find satisfaction in their lives by helping people. They have less interest in our compensation plan, research, conquering mountains, or winning contests and awards. Let's talk about what interests them. That is polite.

Avoid starting off with these phrases when talking to yellow personalities:

- "You must set a goal."
- "You can make a lot of money."

- "Just go out and get 100 no's."

- "Don't take 'no' for an answer."

- "You need to build big."

Here are examples of these phrases that are out-of-synch with the yellow personality.

"You must set a goal now. Nothing worthwhile is achieved without a goal. Write down exactly how many customers and distributors you will commit to signing up during your first 30 days."

"You can make a lot of money, buy a small third-world country, and rule with an iron fist." (Yes, some over-caffeinated red personality leaders will say this when talking to yellow personalities. They forget that not everyone dreams of money and power.)

"Just go out and get 100 no's. Rejection only hurts if you have feelings. Forget your feelings and just tell everyone what we have to offer."

"Don't take 'no' for an answer. The average customer doesn't buy until you have harassed them at least seven times. So keep calling until you break down their willpower and get that order."

"You need to build big. People with small dreams are small people. You don't want to be small, do you?"

Ouch! Maybe these examples are a bit much. However, we should assume that this is what yellow personalities hear when we start with the wrong words.

Phrases for motivation.

All personalities need motivation. It is hard to perform at 100% every day of our lives. We don't have to scream into people's ears like a high school football coach to motivate them. Instead, we can use words that resonate with them. Here are some phrases we can use to help motivate the yellow personalities:

- "By reading this book, it will be easier to connect with people you want to help."
- "By sharing this today, you will encourage others to change their lives."
- "Looking to help more people?"
- "Love giving back to those who need help?"
- "You will love the family feeling of the next big event."
- "Let's make the world a better place."
- "I need your help."
- "Let's do this together."
- "I can feel how much this means to you, and others will feel that too."
- "We want to get everyone we can to the event."

Now, for the examples using these phrases.

"By reading this book, it will be easier to connect with people you want to help. This shows us how to have more pleasant and meaningful conversations with others."

"By sharing this today, you will encourage others to change their lives. You will be planting seeds that will bring happiness and fulfillment to others."

"Looking to help a bunch of people? Here is your chance. This part-time business takes away the money stress from families, and provides them with a better quality of life. Now they have more choices for the future."

"Love giving back to those who need help? You know the old saying, 'Give a man a fish, and he eats for a day. Teach a man to fish, and he eats for a lifetime.' Now your contribution will not only count today, but can change people's lives forever."

"You will love the family feeling of the next big event. We will have a home with this company."

"Let's make the world a better place by sharing our natural, chemical-free cleaning products. No one wants foamy detergents in their local lakes."

"I need your help. If we worked this business part-time, and donated our earnings to the community park fund, we can build the skateboard park in time for summer."

"Let's do this together. We can build this at our own pace, and in a way that is comfortable for us."

"I can feel how much this means to you, and others will feel that too. Let's do this together."

"We want to get everyone we can to the event. For many, this will be a life-changing experience."

Phrases for closing.

Closing can stress yellow personalities. They don't want to push or force their prospects to take action when they are not ready. And what happens when we push and force yellow personalities?

Well, they may not tell us their feelings, but they certainly don't feel good. Yellows are so polite.

We can use the following phrases to help yellow personalities make decisions. The good news is that yellow personalities can use these same phrases when talking to their prospects. It is important for yellow personalities to feel comfortable when talking to others.

- "Start thinking of how many people you can share this with."
- "When would you like to start encouraging others?"
- "With your support, we can work together to impact more lives."
- "I will partner with you, and we can partner with others too."
- "We can do this together."
- "Let's start changing lives ASAP."
- "I can tell that you are looking to help right away."
- "Let's connect tonight at the meeting."

Now for the examples.

"Start thinking of how many people you can share this with. In the beginning, just talk to the people you think it would help the most."

"When would you like to start encouraging others? Why not start now? So many people need encouragement in their lives."

"With your support, we can work together to impact more lives. The two of us could be a great team. We could encourage each other every day to do more to help others."

"I will partner with you, and we can partner with others too. Together we can create a team that connects and improves other people's lives."

"We can do this together. We both want to make a difference. This is our chance to do it."

"Let's start changing lives ASAP. Who can we call first?"

"I can tell that you are looking to help right away. Can we go together to tonight's meeting, so you can start right away?"

"Let's connect tonight at the meeting. I am excited about partnering with you."

When closing with yellow personalities, please remember this. It is difficult for yellow personalities to tell someone "no." They want to be agreeable. They don't want to hurt other people's feelings. Because of their inability to say "no," we must be careful not to take advantage of this. Let's make sure that our yellow personality prospect doesn't feel cornered or obligated.

Phrases for upselling.

Humans tend to think small on new and unknown ventures. We can help people have a bigger commitment and vision.

Sometimes when people join, they have a choice of packages to start their business. The bigger packs have more value, more products to help others, and other additional benefits. The yellow personalities might feel a bit shy about letting others know about the bigger options. They don't want to appear pushy, like a salesman looking to make the biggest sale. Here are some phrases that we can use to help the yellow personality get the bigger sale.

Then, the yellow personalities can use these phrases to comfortably talk to others too.

- "This pack is for helping a few people."
- "This pack is for helping a lot of people."
- "You will help more people with the big pack."
- "How many people would you like to benefit?"
- "Let's make a huge difference."
- "I can feel that you want to make a big impact."
- "This pack can change more lives instantly."
- "We can work together to get this out to everyone."
- "You know you were created to have a profound impact."

Now for the examples.

"This pack is for helping a few people. Now you can change the lives of a few close friends."

"This pack is the recommended pack to help a lot of people. Instead of limiting your help to just a few close friends, you can help even more people improve their lives."

"You will help more people with the big pack. Not only will you have more products to share, but you can pass the discounts along to others."

"How many people would you like to benefit? If you want to benefit more people, you will want the larger pack."

"Let's make a huge difference. With the larger pack, we can help our team have products right away, instead of waiting for them to be shipped."

"I can feel that you want to make a big impact. Can we get the larger pack, with all those extra free products? Then we can use the free products to help new people get started."

"This pack can change more lives instantly. People can immediately experience the products when they hear about them."

"We can work together to get this out to everyone. I know where we can set up at the local market, and this would make a great display."

"You know you were created to have a profound impact. Let's contribute to the world in a meaningful way."

Respect their privacy.

Are yellow personalities outgoing and willing to talk about themselves? Not usually. It is difficult to get them to open up and share their thoughts and feelings. We don't want to rush them before they process our proposals.

Remember, they want to know how their decisions will affect others. That will take some thinking time. And if we aren't a yellow personality, it may be hard to wait for their answers.

Yellow personalities hesitate about setting goals or activating a business plan. But what do the other color personalities say to them? Here is an example of not connecting with a yellow personality:

"You have a plan now. It is called the 40-year-plan. Our plan is better. Why don't you start it now?"

A little rushed. Notice how the focus is on the plan and not the relationship? Yes, this could be communicated better. At the very least, we could give the yellow personality a little more time to process our offer.

How can we improve these conversations?

Use reflective questions.

Here's an example. "You are worried about sending your children to college because it is so expensive. Could you tell me a little bit more about that?"

The yellow personality thinks, "What a great listener."

We built trust quickly. Yellow personalities may like everyone, but they don't necessarily trust everyone. We showed respect to their high-priority concern, their children's education. They feel safer working with people they trust.

Now, as the yellow personality reflects about the expenses of college, they will be selling themselves.

Listen before we talk.

Start our conversations by first being a good listener. Yellow personalities are often interrupted and ignored. We respect them by giving them time to express their feelings and thoughts. Now they will open their minds when it is our turn to talk. We will impress them by giving them our undivided attention, one-on-one, for a few minutes.

Want to destroy this connection? Easy. Be impatient, interrupt them, check our phone messages, and ignore their message.

Our problem is that we have a to-do list that directs us. We focus so much on finishing the items on our to-do list, we fail to be a good listener. Instead, we look for an opening in the conversation to take over and start working on our agenda.

Exhale. Listen first. Then talk. It makes things so much easier.

Speed matters.

Different personalities have different comfort levels with the speed of our conversation. Yellow personalities are more reflective. They want to think about what we say, and also think about their reply. They feel concerned about how their replies might affect other people.

So what will happen if we talk extremely fast to yellow personalities? Will they feel stressed? Certainly. Will they feel rushed? Of course. And now we are taking them outside of their comfort zone.

When people are outside of their comfort zone, our communication suffers. Now they have other concerns besides the words we say. For example, they may wonder if we are talking too fast to hide something. Or, that we are pushing information down their throats with no pauses so they can't interrupt or ask a question.

Yellow personalities need time to understand what we say. They want time to process how they think we feel. That is why we should not rush our conversation, and keep a slow and steady pace.

What about the tone of our voice? Obviously, too loud would not be comfortable. We should keep a more even tone and volume throughout our conversation. No one feels comfortable with wild emotional swings while talking.

Do yellow personalities have objections?

Yes. Here is a quick phrase we can use to start our answer to their objections:

"I know how you feel ..."

These words start the connection. Now we can help the yellow personalities move forward by talking about their concerns.

Here are some examples.

Yellow personality: "I don't have the money in our budget for this now. It is too expensive."

Us: "I know how you feel. We budget every dollar we can for our children and family. But this is a chance to help everyone in our community. You are probably wondering how you can make back your money quickly. Would you like to know how to do this while helping people along the way?"

Another example?

Yellow personality: "I am not a salesman. I don't like selling."

Us: "I know how you feel. You probably want to know how you can share this without being pushy or obnoxious. What if we could focus on helping people instead of trying to sell people?"

Two more examples.

Yellow personality: "I don't have time. I am too busy."

Us: "I know how you feel. Family and obligations take up most of our time. Would you like to know how to help the people in our community with your limited time?"

Yellow personality: "I am not a people person. I am shy. I don't feel comfortable talking to strangers."

Us: "I know how you feel. We want to help people, but we don't want to feel rejected. Would you like to know how to help people without putting pressure on yourself?"

What not to do. A few no-no's.

Avoid violating the values of yellow personalities. They won't compromise on their strong internal values. We can't build trust on violated values.

To understand the personalities better, think of how they prioritize their values. Of the 14 basic values, many yellow personalities would have preferences similar to this.

More prominent values:

- Desire to feel needed.
- Loving relationship with partner.
- Family.
- Personal enlightenment.

Less prominent values:

- Power.
- Financial security.
- Desire to be rich.
- Career fulfillment.
- Desire to look good.
- Adventure junkie.
- Popularity.
- Desire to have a good time.
- Aim for fame.

- Accomplishments.

We should present our offers to support their high-priority values, not to be in conflict with these values.

By knowing which values yellow personalities appreciate more, we can talk to them in a way that will help them feel comfortable. Remember, yellow personalities love stress-free conversations.

What else should we avoid with the yellow personalities?

Avoid rushing decisions, or even rushing replies. Give them time to think about how their answers and decisions will affect the people in their lives.

Avoid focusing on compensation plan details, promises of big money, and recognition awards. Instead, focus on relationships and how we can help others.

And finally, avoid being pushy. This is a great time to be polite.

HOW TO TALK TO BLUE PERSONALITIES.

If you are not familiar with the blue personality, here is a quick overview.

Blues love to party. They love to have fun. Excitement, travel, and trying new things are their priorities. To others, it seems like blues are living their lives at 200 mph with no seatbelt.

And focus? No time for that. It is more fun to switch to new, exciting things.

Blue personalities love to talk to people, especially new people. They will talk to anyone. They talk all the time. That stranger on the elevator that started talking to you? That is a blue personality. Blue personalities talk all day long, and all night long in their sleep.

There is no filter from their brains to their mouths. The blue personalities feel obligated to tell you what they are thinking at every moment. They talk so much that telemarketers will actually hang up on them, and they get banned from talk shows.

We tend to love the blue personalities. They are fun-loving and generally optimistic. They always feel that things will work out. Yes, they don't plan well, but they think quickly on their feet. This makes them the luckiest people we know.

If we have children who are blue personalities, there is never a quiet or boring moment. It seems like the whole world is in action. And while there is plenty of action, there may not be plenty of results.

Trying to communicate with blue personalities? Most of our energy will be spent up front, trying to get their attention. And if this seems exhausting, our next goal is to keep their attention. That is even harder. Why? Because blue personalities live in the moment, and any shiny object or new thought will distract them.

We won't have problems recognizing a blue personality. Of course they are talkative, but they also tend to stand out. They don't hide behind anyone. They will be the ones with the bright Hawaiian shirts, eager to take center stage. To the quieter personalities, it appears that the blue personalities were born to be performers.

So think in terms of fun, and the blue personalities will be our friends. Be prepared for a high-intensity pace with them. We should rest up before we encounter them or they will become energy vampires. We will leave our encounter with a blue personality completely exhausted.

If we are shy, don't worry. They love being the center of attention. No problems with that.

And let's use our common sense. Avoid boring activities like listening to fact-filled business presentations.

The words.

It is easy to recognize blue personalities by the volume of their words. We will also hear specific words in their conversations, messages, and social media posts.

Here are some common words used by blue personalities:

Fun.

Enjoy.

Amusing.

Exciting.

Celebrate.

Laugh.

Holiday.

Party.

Dangerous.

Thrilling.

Entertain.

Interesting.

Awesome.

Incredible.

Unbelievable.

Fast.

Dance.

Mind-boggling.

Surprise.

Shocking.

Expressing.

Perform.

Speaking.

Karaoke.

Escape.

Words like these tip us off that we are in the active world of a blue personality.

What are the blue personalities' priorities?

Fun activities with other people first, tasks second.

The worst punishment in the world for blue personalities? Isolation. Blue personalities are social. Having fun is nice, but it's more fun to have fun with other people. Sharing experiences with others multiplies the fun. And once the experiences are over, blue personalities will spend hours reliving those experiences in conversation with others.

Want to communicate effectively with blue personalities? Then we have to speed up and become more interesting. Of the four different personalities, blue personalities make the quickest decisions. Much of their decision-making centers around this question: "Does this sound interesting and exciting?" If we are not interesting and exciting in the first few seconds, they are gone.

Let's look at some typical phrasing and language examples to help us communicate more effectively.

Prospecting blue personalities.

Remember, short and quick.

- "Do you love to have fun?"
- "You know what is a lot of fun?"
- "This is so exciting."
- "Now this will be really different."
- "Can you picture how much fun we will have?"

- "Can't wait to have fun?"

Here are some examples of these short phrases.

"Do you love to have fun? Are you okay with having fun 24 hours a day? We will do exactly that, starting now."

"You know what is a lot of fun? Meeting new people. Imagine getting paid to meet new people. What could be better than that?"

"This is so exciting. Every day will be a 'wow day' in our business."

"Now this will be really different. You and I hate boring. We will have new experiences every day."

"Can you picture how much fun we will have? New people and new adventures every day."

"Can't wait to have fun? Let's start now, as we both have people we need to talk to."

Phrases for presenting.

With short attention spans and active minds, presentations to blue personalities are a challenge. These small phrases help us keep their attention.

- "Forget the details, let's focus on the fun parts."
- "You will enjoy this part."
- "This is the fun part, talking to others."
- "Looking forward to having a ton of fun in this business?"
- "This will be exciting!"

Let's expand these examples a bit for our presentation.

"Forget the details, let's focus on the fun parts. Can you see yourself talking to new people every day about this business? What could be more fun than that?"

"You will enjoy this part. You love to travel, and we take a lot of trips. How much fun will it be to travel to new locations for holidays with our friends?"

"This is the fun part, talking to others. All we do is talk to others, and the company takes care of all the details."

"Looking forward to having a ton of fun in this business? Let's register now so we can talk to people immediately."

"This will be exciting! I love exciting projects."

We might be tempted to think, "My presentation should be longer." But that is not what our blue personality prospects are thinking. They've already decided if our proposal was fun and interesting or not. Decisions first, details … later? Maybe details … never!

This is a very bad time for a fact-filled presentation. And this is a very good time for us to bite our tongues, as our blue personality prospect is already talking.

We should put our effort into our opening sentences. No need to invest a lot of time in the presentation that will go unheard.

Phrases for selling.

Here is some good news. When we sell products or services to blue personalities, many times our offering is something new. Already we appear interesting. We don't have to go on and on about features, benefits, and unique selling propositions. If our offer is something new, we tell them. If our product does something interesting, we tell them. It is just that simple.

Here are some short phrases that we can use.

- "You will love this."
- "You will be thrilled with the difference."
- "This will make it work even faster."
- "Let's see how fast this works for you."
- "Just try it, you will love it."
- "Super quick and easy."
- "Easy to use, easy to share."
- "It is about results, not boring details."

Now let's put these mini-phrases to work.

"You will love this. Everyone will want to hear your story about this product." (Yeah! I will get a chance to talk more!)

"You will be thrilled with the difference in your utility bill. You will want to tell everyone you know." (I know who I will talk to first. I can't wait for my first bill.)

"This will make it work even faster. You will love the new speed." (Faster? That has to be exciting!)

"Let's see how fast this product works for you. Then you will have the best story ever to tell others." (The best story ever? Wow! I can tell that story over and over.)

"Just try it, you will love it. Why wait?"

"Super quick and easy. Let's start now!"

"Easy to use, easy to share. Let's get to it!"

"It is about results, not boring details. You will love this meeting."

Phrases to avoid.

Any phrase with the word, "data." That would be bad. It doesn't take a rocket scientist to figure out that boring information will drive blue personalities away. Charts, graphs, PowerPoint slides, boring company videos, compensation plan explanations, testimonials, research, and details ... all create tension in our blue personality prospects. They can't wait for us to finish, so they can have a more interesting conversation.

Other color personalities think that blue personalities have a short attention span. But the reality is, they process simple facts and information so quickly, they get bored waiting for us to finish.

Here are some short phrases that ruin our rapport with blue personalities.

- "You need to know all the details."
- "This is important, pay attention."
- "Leveraging your time is important."
- "We have a full training."

We can already feel the conversation going badly. But let's do a few examples using these phrases.

"You need to know all the details. So let's find a date to go to our first class. Then, we can take notes and learn how to implement everything." (Watch the blood slowly drain from the blue personalities' faces.)

"This is important, pay attention. I want to describe the 34 levels of our compensation plan." (Our blue personality prospects are singing songs in their minds, not listening to a word we say.)

"Leveraging your time is important. We need to get a diary and start scheduling everything." (Schedule? The enemy of freedom and having a good time! This almost sounds like discipline.)

"We have a full training starting this Saturday. Come early to get a seat, bring plenty of paper, and by 5pm we will have enough preliminary information so that we can move on to the following week's class."

None of these phrases sound like fun. They certainly aren't exciting. And everything is moving too slowly.

Blue personalities want action.

Phrases for motivation.

Blue personalities love being social. Things are more fun when other people participate.

Do some group activities. This will motivate our blue personality team members, and they will attract other blue personality prospects. Each member of the group feeds off the other members' enthusiasm. Group activities are fun.

Here are some short phrases we can use for motivation.

- "Let's do this now."
- "Our events are like a big party."
- "It will be an awesome time."
- "Can't wait to celebrate when you hit that fun goal."

- "Our group trips are amazing."
- "You will have a blast."
- "Can't wait to party with you."
- "I don't want you to miss out on all the fun."
- "Ready to have some fun?"
- "So excited to have you there."

Here are examples of these mini-phrases at work.

"Let's do this now. Waiting is so boring."

"Our events are like a big party. We meet new people, motivate each other, and have a great time."

"It will be an awesome time. Let's fill the car with new distributors so we can have fun at the event together."

"Can't wait to celebrate when you hit that fun goal. I bet if we talk to twice as many people this week, we will hit that goal before next weekend. That sounds like a great time to announce the party."

"Our group trips are amazing. You don't want to miss a single one. Travel, adventure, and more friends. It doesn't get any better than that."

"You will have a blast. And I am coming with you!"

"Can't wait to party with you. With this new business, we will have so much to talk about."

"I don't want you to miss out on all the fun. Don't be left behind!"

"Ready to have some fun? Let's leave the boring people behind."

"So excited to have you there. And I will introduce you to a lot of new friends."

Phrases for closing.

When we are talking to blue personality prospects, closing is easy. They want to take action. They don't want to sit and analyze things. They think, "Life is meant for living, so let's start living more now."

Want to close our blue personality prospects? Here are a few short phrases to get them to move forward fast.

- "Let's do this tonight."
- "It is exciting once you get started."
- "Let's do this now."
- "This will be a blast."
- "Let's hurry up and get registered so we can ..."
- "It's a quick and easy signup."
- "Let's focus on who we want to have fun with."
- "Who is a ton of fun that we can talk to first?"
- "Excited to have you join."

Notice how we use the word "let's" a lot. Blue personalities like activities that involve other people. They love to be social.

Here are some examples using these small phrases.

"Let's do this tonight. We are action-oriented people."

"It is exciting once you get started. So, let's do this together and have the time of our lives!"

"Let's do this now. Waiting is for boring people."

"This will be a blast. We will have so much fun that we won't even want to sleep."

"Let's hurry up and get registered so we can start qualifying for our first fun trip. We can be roommates at the resort!"

"It's a quick and easy signup. We won't have to wait."

"Let's focus on who we want to have fun with. Who can we call first?"

"Who is a ton of fun that we can talk to first? Our group will be so much fun."

"Excited to have you join. We will get to travel and do so many things together."

Unlike the green personalities, which we will study later in this book, our blue personalities want to take action now. They want instant decisions. No waiting. They think, "I want to sort this out right now."

It is easier for them to make an instant decision now than to wade through boring facts. Think "instant action," and then we can relate to the blue personalities.

Phrases for upselling.

When blue personalities make a decision to join, they want to talk to their friends immediately. No need to wait. If our business offers optional starter packs, here is how to present them to blue personalities.

No need to explain details. Just make the offer.

Here are some example phrases that blue personalities would appreciate.

- "This pack is good if you want to have 'some' fun."
- "This pack is good if you would like to have lots of fun."
- "You will have a ton of fun with the big pack."
- "How many people would you like to talk to?"
- "More samples equals more people we can talk with."
- "Don't worry about the details, this one is more fun."

Here are these phrases in action.

"This pack is good if you want to have 'some' fun. We have enough product to talk to a few people."

"This pack is good if you would like to have lots of fun. We have enough products that we can talk to lots of people immediately."

"You will have a ton of fun with the big pack. Put it by your front door and grab a few products on the way out every morning. What a great way to meet new people."

"How many people would you like to talk to? Everyone? Then the big pack is what we need to start with."

"More samples equals more people we can talk with. What a great way to start conversations."

"Don't worry about the details, this one is more fun. We will use the extra products as prizes at our home presentations. Everyone will be happy they came!"

Do blue personalities have objections?

Yes. But remember, they don't hold a single thought very long. We don't want to overdo our answers.

Need some great first words to say when blue personalities have objections? Say:

"I get it."

Be quick, talk fast, and don't make them wait. Here are some quick examples.

Objection: "I don't want to sit in Saturday's training. It is so boring."

Our response: "I get it. We don't want to be bored. But you will meet so many new people there, and that will be exciting."

Objection: "Follow-up is boring. I would rather meet new people."

Our response: "I get it. But it is fun when they join. Why not tell them about the new trip when you call them?"

Objection: "It is no fun being a pushy salesman."

Our response: "I get it. What if we focused on the fun parts instead of the traditional sleazy sales tactics?"

Objection: "I can't remember all that stuff to do a presentation."

Our response: "I get it. Presentations are boring. Nobody wants to listen to them anyway. Only talk about the parts that you find most interesting."

The good news is that blue personalities don't have many objections. For example, you will never hear a blue personality say, "I don't want to go to the event." Never happens. Why? Because events are fun. They are like parties. New people, a chance to chat with everyone, new experiences. If the event is far away, it is the same as an exciting road trip!

Speed matters.

Blue personalities? They are tornados of communication. Unbridled speed, wild changes of subjects, and no time to listen to us talk.

Yes, communicating with blue personalities will be a challenge. We must limit ourselves to short bits of information and very short sentences. Because blue personality brains work at hyperspeed, they want to finish our sentences for us. They want to answer our questions before we even ask the questions. The problem is that they can listen and process many times faster than we can speak. Conversation can be boring for blue personalities.

If you are not sure if some of your prospects are blue personalities, give this test. Try a short conversation, and see how fast they reply. Blue personalities reply instantly. They won't take time to think and consider what we said. Instead, they react.

To understand the blue personalities better, let's do a little game. Now, this game will be fun for us, but torture for blue personalities. Here is what we are going to do.

#1. Start our sentence to the blue personalities very slowly. As we progress through the sentence, go even slower. Then leave pauses between each word.

#2. Watch the blue personalities twitch, bite their lips, get tense, and finally break down, interrupt us, and finish the sentence for us. They can't stand the suspense.

So when we talk to blue personalities, we need to speed up. A good plan is to have a few cups of coffee before talking to them. Maybe jump up and down, listen to motivational music, or do whatever it takes to increase our metabolism and accelerate our speech.

Our goal is to communicate with them in the best possible way so they hear our message. That means talk fast, talk short, and be ready for them to interrupt and take over the conversation at their first chance. This means we want our best information very early in our conversation.

What not to do. A few no-no's.

Don't force blue personalities to plan, plan, and plan some more. Their personality craves making instant decisions, and then going into action. Trapping them into a long-term plan feels restrictive. We might think, shouldn't they plan more? No.

Blue personalities are innovative. They're lucky, and always seem to land on their feet. They always seem to come up with creative last-minute solutions to offset their lack of planning.

So long-term planning, step-by-step processes, and checklists are not natural for the blue personalities. Let's allow them to shine with their quick thinking and spur-of-the-moment adjustments.

What if we need more blue personalities on our team?

If our goal is to get into momentum, then yes, blue personalities can help us get there. Here is how we can locate blue personalities for our team right away.

Go up to anyone and ask a simple question: "Who do you know that is a good storyteller?"

This question is not invasive or scary. Most people can refer us to a good storyteller. Naturally, this person will be a blue personality.

Then, all we have to do is call this referral. Our phone call might go something like this:

"Hi John. Your friend, Mary, said that you were a good storyteller. Is that true?"

If the person gives us a "yes" answer, we can say:

"There are two types of storytellers in the world. Those who tell stories, and those who tell stories and get paid for it."

That is all we have to say. The blue personality can sort out if now is the time to start getting paid for telling stories, or to continue telling stories for free.

Want a deeper understanding of why blue personalities do the things they do?

To understand the blue personalities better, think of how they prioritize their values. Of the 14 values, many blue personalities would have preferences similar to this.

More prominent values:

- Desire to look good.
- Loving relationship with partner.
- Family.
- Personal enlightenment.
- Adventure junkie.

- Popularity.
- Desire to have a good time.

Less prominent values:

- Power.
- Financial security.
- Desire to be rich.
- Career fulfillment.
- Desire to feel needed.
- Aim for fame.
- Accomplishments.

We can connect with the blue personalities more effectively when we know what they value most. This helps us hold their attention. It is more fun talking to blue personalities when we are heard.

How to talk to red personalities.

"Hurry up. You better be quick. Get to the point or you are toast!" Red personalities don't have time for idle chit-chat.

Red personalities live to achieve. They are the doers. They get things done and measure their results. If they are not the boss, you can guarantee they think they are smarter than their boss. Think of the red personalities as confident, extroverted, impatient for results, and very decisive. It doesn't take much time for them to make a decision and get into action. They will have a plan, and the focus to achieve it.

Leadership? Yes, red personalities want to be leaders, want to be in charge, and are great organizers who get things done. Having this strong will helps them set goals, focus, and achieve those goals. The downside is that the red personalities resist listening to alternate viewpoints. Our suggestions are generally ignored.

But it is this same ego that helps red personalities shrug off rejection. They think, "It is okay if you don't like me or what I offer. I am not responsible for you having bad taste."

Please note that the Earth does not revolve around the sun. The Earth revolves around the red personality. 110% of everything we say should be all about "what's in it for them."

Red personalities assume they are the "alpha" of any group. Because of this, they don't take criticism well and take offense at conflicting beliefs.

The yellow and blue personalities think about the relationship first, and the task second. Red personalities are the opposite. They think about achieving the task first, and the relationship second. To others, red personalities appear a bit unsympathetic or cold, because their focus is on completing the task in the most efficient way possible.

Some examples of red personalities? Successful politicians, trial lawyers, athletes who showboat, and anyone on social media who loves to show off. Yes, they are easy to spot.

The words.

Words will help us recognize people with red personality traits. We will hear these words, see these words in messages, and notice these words in their social media posts.

Here are some common words used by red personalities.

Dominate.

Power.

Authority.

Leadership.

Wealth.

Win.

Compete.

Challenge.

Achieve.

Accomplish.

Success.

Perform.

First-class.

Boss.

Influence.

Control.

Goals.

Big.

Command.

Manage.

Fast.

Recognition.

Focus.

Build.

When we hear words such as these, this tips us off that we could be talking to a red personality.

What are the red personalities' priorities?

Tasks first, people and relationships second.

Red personalities get the job done. If we have a project that needs to be completed, they will set goals, focus, plan, and execute.

"What's in it for me?" is their motto, so we know what to focus on.

Conversation? Don't worry if they interrupt us. Red personalities already know the answer and can't waste time with our chit-chat.

The most important word is the word "you." We must focus on them and limit the use of the word "I," because it doesn't apply to them.

Red personalities seem money-driven because it is a way to keep score. Sure, they will build relationships, if it is quick and will benefit them. But keeping score? That is important. To red personalities, results matter the most.

Want an instant connection with red personalities? Talk to their egos. Like everyone, they love it when we talk about them. And if we tell them how great they are, they won't disagree.

Empathy?

Don't expect red personalities to have empathy. Remember their priorities? Tasks and projects first. They don't worry about how difficult it was to come visit them, or how bad the traffic was for us. But the good news is that they don't expect empathy from us either. They just want to talk about the task at hand.

We don't have to worry about long talks about our personal lives, chit-chatting about current events, and building a feel-good relationship.

Red personalities are thinking, "Just get to the point. Now." If we delay the reason for our conversation, we create tension and impatience.

Red personality language examples.

Red personalities prejudge us also, and they can be harsh. The less like them we are, the worse the prejudgment. We want to talk to them quickly and directly. They are comfortable with that approach.

If we talk in the red language, we make it easier for red personalities to understand our intentions. These examples help us focus on their desire for results.

- "Here is how we will do this."

- "Bottom line? Here is how this works."

- "If Barry can do it, you will do it twice as fast."

- "You will be at the top in record time."

- "This is what you are best at. Let's get started."

- "You will be #1."

- "This plan is for doers, not watchers."

We don't have to cushion our words. Get to the point. Red personalities don't want to sit and listen. They want to take action.

Focus.

First, the facts. Red personalities want to know the bottom line. There is no time for the back story. If we want to describe research to the red personalities … don't! They only want to know the results. If we want to describe a problem? Don't. They only want to know if we are going to take action to fix it.

To get red personalities to listen to us, here are some tips.

- What are the facts and how do the facts apply to them?
- How much money is involved? Can they earn a lot?
- How can they earn this money?
- What is the first step they can take right now?
- What does it take to get to the top?
- Who is the competition?
- Oh yeah, and what are we selling again?

Very direct. No need for additional fluff and information that doesn't matter. Let's get to the point and keep the focus on them.

Phrases for presenting.

Like most people, red personalities think about themselves. We have to interrupt their thinking to get their attention.

Here are some opening lines to get their attention.

- "Interested in earning more than your boss?"
- "Want to get paid for how much you actually do?"
- "Are they paying you what you are worth?"
- "Interested in making more money than your friends? Then this is your plan."
- "Want to get the recognition you deserve?"
- "Want to be in charge?"
- "Looking to win?"

Now that we have their attention, we have to act fast. Here are some examples of these phrases in use.

"Interested in earning more than your boss? Here is the bottom line. Our income won't change unless we do something different. Let's start this business now."

"Want to get paid for how much you actually do? Now you will get paid what you are worth, not what somebody else thinks you are worth. Watch how big your paycheck will be when you get rewarded fairly."

"Are they paying you what you are worth? Of course not. You deserve more. Here is how you can get it."

"Interested in making more money than your friends? Then, this is your plan. You can write your own paycheck."

"Want the recognition you deserve? You can be #1 and the superstar that everyone looks up to. You were born to win, so this feels natural for you."

"Want to be in charge? Now you can be your own boss. You call the shots. You are in control. And you determine how big your paycheck will be."

"Looking to win? Now you can control your results. You will love this."

Phrases for selling.

If we are selling products or services to a red personality, here are some phrases we can use.

- "It is a luxury product."
- "Anyone who is anyone wants this."
- "No one wants to go second class."
- "People expect you to have the best."

- "You deserve the best."

- "You are smart. You see the value."

Talking to red personalities? Teaching them to sell to others? Here are these sample phrases in action.

"It is a luxury product. No one wants to represent cheap junk."

"Anyone who is anyone wants this. You will know exactly which people to talk to."

"No one wants to go second class. Give them the choice of first class."

"People expect you to have the best. This will show them why you are #1."

"You deserve the best. People look up to you."

"You are smart. You see the value. I don't have to explain anything else."

Phrases to avoid.

How do red personalities see the world? They see tasks and projects to accomplish. Goals to reach. They keep scorecards on how well they do, and how quickly they accomplish their tasks.

We want to talk to them in a way that stays in line with their view of the world. There will be a disconnect with the red personalities if we use phrases such as these:

- "It is all about sharing and caring."

- "You must personally connect with the person first."

- "It is all about helping others, not you."

- "You need to be a great listener."

- "We want to bond with our prospects."

How about a few slightly exaggerated examples?

"You have to personally connect with the prospect first, so set aside time for chit-chat and bonding."

"It is about helping others, not you. So let's have a group hug session first before we meditate on how this will affect others."

"You need to be a great listener. Set aside some time to sit and listen to people first. When they finish talking, then you can begin sharing your message."

"We want to bond with our prospects. They need to feel our positive vibrations and connection to the universe. Once they sense the power of our aura, they can levitate gently to the horizon of awareness." (Yeah, way over the top exaggeration. Red personalities want action and results. To them, setting aside valuable business time to build personal relationships is bad time management.)

Phrases for motivation.

The nature of a red personality is to be competitive. If there is a contest, they want to win it. If there is recognition, they want it. If there is a trophy, they need their name on that trophy. Recognition is a high priority for red personalities.

Red personalities seldom need extra motivation. Their personal goals make them self-motivated. But if we want to add a bit of fuel to the fire, here are some phrases that we can use.

- "Since you are a real leader, you will be the first to get your event ticket."

- "I know you are 'on it' already."

- "If he can do it, I am sure you can make this happen."
- "No one wants to come in second place."
- "You are the winner. Go for it."
- "You are smart, so I know you will be there."
- "All the leaders will be there."
- "I don't want someone else to beat you to it."

Now for some sample phrases.

"You are a real leader. Your team expects to see you on the front row."

"I know you are 'on it' already. You and I don't have time to chat about it."

"If he can do it, I am sure you can make this happen. You will do it in half the time."

"No one wants to come in second place. Why bother competing if we don't want to win?"

"You are a winner and will go to the top fast. You might even set a record for the fastest person to achieve this level."

"You are smart, so I know you will be there. This is a great chance to build faster."

"All the leaders will be there. You will want to see how they are doing."

"I don't want someone else to beat you to it. Let's act now."

Most red personalities are so competitive that they can't play a game without keeping score. Everything turns into a contest. If we wanted our red personalities to bring more people to our opportunity meetings, all we would have to do is say, "Last week, Mary brought three guests to our meeting. I am not sure you could bring that many." Those are "fighting words" to red personalities. They cannot resist. They have to take up the challenge.

Once we understand their competitive nature, it is easy to consistently motivate the red personality. Imagine we are sitting at a convention with our red personality distributor. All we would have to say is, "I know you want to be on stage next year getting your recognition. You don't want to be sitting in the audience, clapping for your friends as they walk across the stage." Our red personality distributor can't wait to leave the convention and start building faster.

Phrases for closing.

Red personalities are closers. They want decisions now. They have no patience for people who dawdle and want to think it over.

Their focus is on the sale. They want to know if the prospect will move forward now, or not. They don't take rejection personally, because it is all about the task at hand. Their closing statements are direct and to the point. So, they expect our closing statement to them to be equally direct.

Here are some statements.

- "You can easily crush it."
- "Can you see how you will quit your job?"
- "Ready to start planning how you will customize your new car?"
- "You already know who you will bring into the business."
- "Here is your chance to lead."

- "You are smart, so I don't have to sell you on this."

- "Honestly, you have more talent than the top earners."

- "I am sure you are ready and not looking to settle."

- "So who should we invite to be on your team?"

- "Let's make you profitable right away."

Now for the examples.

"You can easily crush it. This is easy for leaders."

"Can you see how you will quit your job? We will follow this plan to make sure we match your current income fast."

"Ready to start planning how you will customize your new car? You will qualify at the highest bonus level and have the company pay for your luxury car."

"You already know who you will bring into the business. Let's get them started right away. Then we will look for other builders."

"Here is your chance to lead. People respect that you move forward while everyone else waits."

"You are smart, so I don't have to sell you on this. You can see that this is what we should do."

"Honestly, you have more talent then the top earners. Here is your chance to use your talent and have everyone see the results."

"I am sure you are ready and not looking to settle. Life isn't over yet. Let's do something now."

"So who should we invite to be on your team? Let's choose the best people first."

"Let's make you profitable right away. Bottom line, this is about earning big money."

Don't be afraid to be direct. We won't hurt the red personalities' feelings. In fact, they will enjoy a simple closing statement so that they can make a decision. We could say, "You seem to enjoy what I showed you. This will be good for you. So why not give it a try right now?"

Or, we could say, "You don't have any more questions. You have all the facts. This solves your problem. So let's get started now."

To the other color personalities, this might seem too cold and direct. But remember, the red personalities are focused on the task, and they want to make a decision.

Phrases for upselling.

When red personalities make the decision to join, they want to get into action immediately. If our business offers optional starter packs, here is how to present them to red personalities.

This is our time to be very direct with them. Point out the options. Then, recommend the larger options. Red personalities don't think small, and they don't want to start small. We don't have to be shy.

Here are some example phrases that red personalities would appreciate.

- "This pack is good if you want to make 'some' money."
- "This pack is good if you would like to make a ton of money."
- "You will make more money with the big pack."

- "How many people would you like on your team?"
- "No one wants a small business."
- "This is for the go-getters."
- "The leaders get this pack."
- "The bigger the pack, the bigger the profit."

Let's put these phrases to use.

"This pack is good if you want to make 'some' money. But, I know you didn't join to have a small business."

"This pack is good if you would like to make a ton of money. Let's start with this and build the biggest bonus check we can."

"You will make more money with the big pack. The profits are better, and we can get people started faster."

"How many people would you like on your team? Let's get enough product to start your potential leaders so they can help you build."

"No one wants a small business. Let's invite as many people as we can to your home launch meeting."

"This is for the go-getters. The other packs are for the hobbyists."

"The leaders get this pack. The followers get those packs."

"The bigger the pack, the bigger the profit. So I know which pack you want."

Challenges!

Red personalities love challenges. Here is what they are thinking:

"Want to go for the record?" Yes.

"Do you think you can do this?" Yes.

"Can you see yourself at the top?" Yes.

"Do you think you can earn a promotion to Diamond before July?" Yes.

The thrill of achieving is everything to red personalities. Let's give them the pleasure and satisfaction of achieving something big.

Weak is bad.

When we appear weak, red personalities will not respect our message. The solution? We need to boost our self-confidence. While it may take months or years of personal development to do that, there is a shortcut. We simply talk confidently. This requires changing a few words of our current vocabulary.

Here are some weak words:

Could.

Try.

Might.

Probably.

Instead of using these words, why not replace them with words that feel more powerful and certain?

Here are some examples.

Before: "This could get our prospects excited."

After: "This will get our prospects excited."

Before: "Let's try this."

After: "Let's do this."

Before: "This might work."

After: "This works."

Before: "We could probably make Level 4 before the end of the month."

After: "We will crush Level 4 before this month ends."

Red personalities don't want to hear words such as "maybe" or "possibly." There is nothing tentative about their actions. If we talk with authority, they will listen.

We don't want to be arrogant or appear aggressive. However, we do want to show our conviction for what we say. Red personalities respect someone with strong beliefs.

If we want to add a little bit of body language, here are a few quick things we can do.

Sit up straight. Hold our heads high. And avoid fidgeting with our hands. If this is a problem, make sure we have a prop or something to hold onto that looks natural. And it doesn't hurt to have our shoulders back. This body language will make us look more influential and confident.

Need more confidence?

Then, we must practice what we say. Why? So what we say sounds confident without a lot of conversation fillers. What are conversation fillers? These are tiny words or phrases we say to fill in the gaps or empty spaces in our conversation. Some examples?

"I mean …"

"Well, uh, uh ..."

"You know ..."

"Like, uh ..."

If we practice what we say, we won't need these conversation fillers. Our audience senses that we have conviction.

Confidence is contagious. People want to follow people who know where they are going, and have the confidence to get there.

Speed matters.

Think about this. Do red personalities like to talk, or listen? This is an easy question. Of course, red personalities want to do all of the talking. They have all the best ideas, they are right all the time, and they need to tell us about it. They want to tell us how to run our lives, what to buy, and what to do.

So when we are talking to red personalities, we want to be efficient. We won't have much time, so we want to get our best ideas in quickly. Red personalities are very direct. They want the bottom line, without much description and fanfare. Just get to the point.

So what should our speed be when talking to red personalities? Obviously very fast. They want us to finish our part of the conversation quickly, so they can get back to talking.

Remember the game we played with the blue personalities? The game where we talked very slowly until the blue personalities couldn't stand it any longer? If we play the same game with the red personalities, we get the same results. They don't need to think about what we say. They will have a response ready for us before we finish our last word.

To make our communication work with red personalities, we are the ones that have to adjust. We want to talk faster, but make sure we have pertinent and direct information. To do this, we should prepare a bit in advance. Let's think about our most interesting and best points, and then try to say them all in the first few sentences.

Stressing red personalities with slow and deliberate speech is not a good plan. Our best communication with them will come from us adjusting our speed to their speed.

Do red personalities have objections?

Yes. These objections will be direct and strong. It will be difficult to change the red personalities' minds, so we have to make the new viewpoint their idea. We can answer their objections starting with this key phrase:

"I agree."

People feel better when we agree with them. We do not want to argue with red personalities. Here are some examples of using "I agree" to answer objections.

Objection: "I don't have time to follow up with people who can't make up their minds."

Our response: "I agree. You don't have time for people who can't make a quick decision. I see why you didn't follow up with them. We can assign that task to someone on your team."

Objection: "I can make more money now by buying and selling properties. Why should I do this?"

Our response: "I agree. You can't make big up-front money here like you can flipping properties. But this gives you the cash flow you need to live between property deals."

Objection: "I don't want to spend that kind of money for a startup kit and inventory."

Our response: "I agree, you want to make money, not spend money. Would you like to know how to turn a big profit with this startup pack right away?"

Start with the "I agree" phrase. We have to have an audience. Red personalities stop listening and argue with us if we don't respect their objections.

What not to do. A few no-no's.

Don't offer unsolicited advice. Ever.

Even if red personalities ask for advice, beware. It is a trap. They only want confirmation for what they are going to do anyway. Red personalities know everything, so our low-level, inaccurate advice is unwelcome.

Do red personalities know everything? According to them, yes. They probably have a sign above their desk that quotes Isaac Asimov:

"People who think they know everything are a great annoyance to those of us who do."

Okay. A little harsh. But it is this attitude that gives the red personalities the confidence to move forward and take control of the situation. When we put the odds in their favor in our presentation, their response is quick and decisive. They are ready for immediate action.

Want to make the call to action clearer for the red personalities? Then include the "endgame" or goal. Once they know the final goal, they immediately start planning the steps to get there.

Want agreement and action? Then, it is a good idea to make everything seem like it was their idea. Red personalities want control of their circumstances and surroundings. They want to stand out and not be a faceless member of the crowd.

What if we are not as motivated or as disciplined as our red personality prospects?

They will notice. And their respect for our suggestions or proposals will be low. At the very least, we should have the discipline to prepare an organized presentation. Small talk, frivolous conversation, and a wandering focus will mean that we are talking, but our audience has gone home.

Want a deeper understanding of why red personalities do the things they do?

To understand red personalities better, think of how they prioritize their values. Of the 14 values, many red personalities would have preferences similar to this.

More prominent values:

- Desire to look good.

- Power.

- Desire to be rich.

- Career fulfillment.

- Aim for fame.

- Accomplishments.

- Adventure junkie.

Less prominent values:

- Popularity.

- Desire to have a good time.

- Financial security.

- Desire to feel needed.

- Loving relationship with partner.

- Family.

- Personal enlightenment.

So, when we are talking about becoming rich or being #1, the red personalities pay attention. For them, maybe we shouldn't call these values, but should call them motivators.

It is difficult to get red personalities to listen to us. Their patience lasts only a few seconds. Our solution is to make sure our conversation focuses on these red personality values.

How to talk to green personalities.

If we are not familiar with the green personality, here is a quick overview.

Green personalities tend to be quieter, more reserved, and focused on facts and information. When we ask them a question, they will pause to consider their answer. They are thinking of the different possible answers and the information they will need to make sure that their response will be accurate.

Think of green personalities as engineers, accountants, data processing professionals, and the emotionless Mr. Spock from *Star Trek*. Yes, this is an exaggeration. However, it forces us to focus on details and information. Now we are connecting with the green personalities. We are speaking their language.

We should talk to green personalities about being thrifty, paying off the house, and getting a good return on our investment.

Social time? Not the most comfortable activity for green personalities. For some extreme green personalities, their social interaction will follow this pattern:

Thin smile, and a nod to acknowledge our presence.

Mumble, "Hmmm."

Shrug shoulders at appropriate moments.

Check phone for possible (but unlikely) messages from others.

Sip drink nervously.

Look for a corner to hide in and surf the Internet.

Bottom line: We can avoid chit-chat and pleasantries. Instead, communicate about facts and information.

The words.

What are some examples of the words green personalities would use? Here are some common ones.

Instructions.

Data.

Science.

Facts.

Information.

Details.

Bottom line.

Numbers.

Research.

Analyze.

Proof.

Fact-finding.

Criteria.

Reason.

Why.

Study.

Experiment.

Testing.

When we hear these words, we know we are talking to a green personality who insists, "Give me the facts. Just the facts, please." This sounds boring to non-green personalities.

Facts first. And then more facts.

Green personalities don't have time to think about feelings and social niceties. Their entire attention is on the facts. Get the information right, and then it will be easy for them to make a decision.

Breaking the ice, warming the relationship, creating rapport, and other social conversation-starters have less effect with green personalities. They ignore most of this activity so that they can focus on the facts and information.

Like red personalities, green personalities want us to get to the point.

But there is a bigger problem we need to address first. Here it is.

Green personalities worry.

They suffer from the "crack in the dam" worry program. Here is an example.

Imagine we are green personalities. We want to buy a house. The agent takes us to a beautiful neighborhood, and shows us the perfect house. Enough bedrooms? Yes. Enough bathrooms? Yes. The neighborhood schools are great? Yes. The neighbors? The friendliest people we ever met.

Everything is perfect except one little thing. When we look out of the back window of our potential dream home, we notice a large dam. In one corner of the dam there are small cracks. We ask the agent, "Does this dam hold a lot of water?" The agent replies, "Yes. It holds the water for the entire city."

We then ask the agent, "Do you see those small cracks over in the corner of the dam?" He replies, "Yes. Those cracks have been there a long time. Don't worry about them."

Later we return home to think about this home. What do we think about the most? Yes, the cracks in the dam. We worry that if we buy this home, we might be making a huge mistake. Everything else is perfect. But even though the agent assured us that those small cracks were nothing unusual, we continue to worry about those cracks in the dam.

What happens? We eventually look for another house. We give up on our dream house and buy a house that is inferior, but we feel safe that we did not make a bad decision.

And this is how green personalities think.

We can show green personalities the most incredible opportunity in the world. But a single tiny flaw will hold their attention and prevent them from moving forward. When prospecting and presenting to green personalities, we must keep their fear of bad decisions in mind.

Instead of spending a long time on the features and benefits of our program, we will shift more time and focus to showing how safe it will be to work with us.

The fear of making a mistake dominates the green personality thinking. We must show green personalities that we have thought through the potential problems, and that the decision to move forward with us is safe.

We will prepare ourselves for even the tiniest objection. An unsatisfactory answer to a small problem will block green personalities from moving forward. We have to address any and all problems satisfactorily.

How do we do this? We look at our offer from the viewpoint of a negative skeptic. Think of all the problems or questions a negative prospect will have. Then, we create logical answers to these potential objections.

Now, our presentation to green personalities will mention potential concerns and how we are prepared to take care of them. The green personalities feel secure. They respect that we talk their language.

Green personalities get a bad reputation. Presenters say, "They take forever to make up their minds. They delay, research, and put off their decisions forever." Well, that is true if we do not give a complete presentation that addresses potential problems and concerns.

But surprise! When we show green personalities that we predicted their potential concerns, and we took care of those issues, they will make a quick decision.

Green personalities are not procrastinators. They simply want to make sure they don't make a mistake by moving forward. They are thorough in their research, and worry about unseen or unknown potential problems. By anticipating their objections, we will impress them with our thoroughness.

Let's look at a few short examples.

Example #1. Imagine that we sell skincare.

To start in our business, a new distributor would buy a complete demo skincare and makeup kit for $300. What concerns do we think green personalities would have about making this purchase?

"What if no one wants to buy skincare and makeup from me?"

"What if I start this business and fail?"

"What if my friends tell me I made a bad decision?"

If we wait for green personalities to verbalize these questions, we will be on the defensive and look unprepared. But as professionals, we anticipate their questions. Our presentation will bring up these potential problems and objections first. We look impressive.

We might say,

"As a new distributor you can buy $400 worth of skincare and makeup for only $300. That is a great business decision that will save you money. You might also worry that no one wants to buy skincare and makeup from your business. Or worse yet, what if this business is not for you? Or, what if your friends tell you that you made a bad decision? Don't worry. We have three safety nets to protect you from any risk.

"First, our company has a 100% money back guarantee on your $300 purchase. You will never risk losing a single cent.

"The second safety net you have is me. As your sponsor, I am responsible to make sure you have a successful start to your business. As you know, I have experience and do this every day. I will partner with you. I will help you get customers and sell products until you are on your third re-order. This guarantees you have a solid business."

"And third, even if no one buys a single item, you could use these products yourself over the next several months. As you mentioned before, you love these products. This is a great way to get them at a huge discount."

How will our green personalities feel? Fantastic. With their security issues gone, it is easy for them to make a logical decision to join. They save money on their personal skincare and makeup. They have zero risk.

Example #2. Motivate green personalities to attend our company convention.

What concerns would they have?

Airfare and hotel expenses.

Missing one day of work or losing a vacation day.

Feeling uncomfortable with all the hype at the convention.

As pros, we anticipate these concerns and have this discussion with our green personalities.

"Attending our annual convention is a smart business move. First, the entire trip is tax-deductible. We want to take advantage of our business tax benefits. At the convention, we will associate with like-minded distributors. We will talk, discuss, and exchange ideas on our favorite subject, our business. One good idea will pay for our entire trip. Third, by taking Friday off from our jobs, we will have a three-day weekend together. I can't wait for the deep conversations we will have with the other serious distributors."

By addressing the green personalities' concerns first, we don't allow them to look for reasons not to go. Instead, we turn their potential objections into reasons to go to our convention.

Example #3. The reluctant customer.

Imagine we sell electricity. Our green personality customers are afraid of change. Change brings the unknown into the immediate future. That means risk. And risk means the potential for a bad decision.

Bad decisions! Yikes. That is why green personalities research. They want to avoid bad decisions.

What is the initial reaction from green personalities? Avoid change. Stay on the current course. The present is a known commodity that is safe.

Here is where we can make a bad decision. If we decide to motivate our green personalities by giving them the benefits of changing, they will resist. Their issue is not with a lack of benefits. Their fear is that by changing, they will be making a mistake.

The solution? Concentrate on the safety of making a change. This is the big decision point for our green personality friends.

Here is an example of "missing the point" and talking about benefits to green personalities.

"When you change to our electricity service, we shop for the lowest rates daily on the open market. Our specialized electricity buyers constantly search for the best price for your home. This allows us to have an average bill that is 2.5% lower than our competitors. So do you want to change to us?"

Could there be some unverbalized fears and objections from our green personality prospects? Of course. What types of fears would hold them back from making a decision?

What if the new electricity supplier goes out of business? Will I be cut off?

What if the service is substandard?

What if the fine print on this new contract allows them to supersize my bill?

Who will fix my electricity after a storm?

Let's see what we could say to green personalities to alleviate their fears. This would be a better conversation.

"Everyone gets the same electricity on our national grid. Nothing will change. Same electricity. Same service. Same repairmen. The only thing that will change is that we send you a slightly lower bill. There is no need for you to continue over-paying for your current service. We will fix that for you."

Now we have eliminated the fear of change.

"If/then" statements.

"If/then" statements work great with green personalities. This is a comfortable way for green personalities to assimilate new ideas and information. Use these statements to bypass the natural skepticism of our green personality prospects. Some examples?

"If you purchase the premium pack, then you will get the biggest discount."

"If you invite 20 friends to your business launch, then you can expect five friends to come. It is unrealistic to believe that everyone will have the same day and time free on their calendar."

"If you use this cream for 21 days, then you will see a massive difference in your skin."

"If you attend this weekend's fast-start training, then you will leave with better invitation and presentation skills."

"If you don't notice a difference in 30 days, then call me and I will arrange an instant refund."

"If you present our business as an option to your friends, then you will never have to worry about rejection."

"If you like saving money on your taxes, then you will love being in business for yourself. Our government gives tax breaks to businesses because it helps the economy."

"If you delay starting your business, then you will miss out on this month's special offer."

"If you start your business now, then we can start the countdown to firing your boss."

"If/then" statements make it easy for green personalities to take action. They know what will happen next, and that feels great.

Don't talk about benefits.

Green personalities focus more on the safety of the offer, and less on the excitement of the offer. Too much excitement or hype pushes green personalities away. It triggers their "too good to be true" program. This creates skepticism. And that means no decision.

When green personalities hear something great, their first reaction is, "What is the catch?" This is an automatic response.

Facts help us reduce the appearance of hype.

But what is even more important than facts? The "appearance" of true facts.

Even though what we say can be verified and proven, if it appears "too good to be true," green personalities will resist. It is better to restrain our excitement or even point out slight flaws in our offer. Here is an example of helping our green personalities believe our offer.

"Our testimonials praise the surge of energy they get from our vitamins. However, we know that nothing works 100% of the time for 100% of the people. So it is possible that someone may not feel the tremendous surge of energy others report. For these rare people, we offer our instant 100% money-back guarantee. We only want super-satisfied customers for our business."

For green personalities, the "removal of risk" is far more important than benefits.

We should focus our presentation on the safety of the decision. For our green personalities, "no risk" means an intelligent decision.

Do green personalities want to know how we feel?

Not really. Yellow personalities want to know how we feel. Now, this is not to say that green personalities are emotionless or insensitive. However, when we talk to green personalities, their brains are busy processing the facts. Remember, they want to focus on the task at hand and make sure that the solution is correct.

So we could say this to the green personality:

"I hurt my finger yesterday, so it was difficult to drive here. While driving, I realized I forgot my wallet. Thank goodness I wasn't stopped by the police, as I didn't have my driver's license. Anyway, the traffic wasn't so bad. Now, let me show you this business I mentioned on the phone. Our company was started in 1999. That was the same year my daughter was born. It doesn't seem that long ago."

Here is what the green personality heard:

"Our company was started in 1999."

While we are chit-chatting and attempting to build rapport, the green brain is waiting for facts to process. We have to remember that green personalities will focus on information.

The good news is that all the mini-traumas in life are completely ignored by the green personalities. They are looking at our opportunity and products based on their own merits.

Green personality language examples.

If we talk in the "green" language, we make it easier for green personalities to understand our message.

These examples help us focus on delivering the information and facts.

- "It just makes sense."
- "Let's figure this out."
- "Here is proof."

- "The test results show …"
- "Numbers can't lie."

Oh, these phrases are music to the ears of green personalities. Let's use these phrases in some examples.

"It just makes sense to buy it wholesale. We can put the savings right in our pocket."

"Let's figure this out. If we can continue our current pace, we can replace our full-time income in only four more months."

"Here is proof. These four engineers put the products through rigorous testing, and reported their findings."

"The test results show how fast this works in real life. Our customers will be thrilled."

"Numbers can't lie. We will never get rich by working this job. We must do something different."

Phrases for presenting.

What kind of words and phrases would green personalities enjoy when they look at our business opportunity? Here are a few.

- "Want to leverage your efforts?"
- "Want to increase your tax deductions?"
- "This is the easiest way to add a second income."
- "Let's figure out how to get rid of debt so we can invest more."
- "You can easily see how much we can earn in our first month."

Now let's expand these phrases.

"Want to leverage your efforts? Let's get our first two people immediately. Then there will be three people building on the team."

"Want to increase your tax deductions? Let's start our business immediately to get today's tax deductions."

"This is the easiest way to add a second income. No waiting for part-time job interviews. We can start making money immediately."

"Let's figure out how to get rid of debt so we can invest more. This business helps pay off and eliminate debt."

"You can easily see how much money we can earn in our first month with the fast-start plan."

Phrases for selling.

- "Research shows how much we will benefit."
- "It has been tested."
- "You will actually save money."
- "Here is the proof."
- "There have been many studies on this."
- "5 out of 5 _____ recommend this."
- "Every professional _____ agrees."
- "They went above and beyond to prove the benefits."

Let's put these magical phrases to work.

"Research shows how much we benefit by reducing our utility bills by as little as $25 a month."

"It has been tested in over 30 studies. The benefits are well-documented."

"You will actually save money by using these products. It is like putting extra money into the bank."

"Here is the proof. It is irrefutable."

"There have been many studies on this. It is good backup information when we talk to people."

"5 out of 5 investment advisors recommend this."

"Every professional in the association agrees."

"They went above and beyond to prove the benefits. Look at these amazing documented results."

Phrases for motivation.

Oh. This is going to be hard. Why? Because green personalities operate on logic first. Most motivational or hype phrases won't have the effect we want. But, let's do the best we can.

- "You already know this makes sense."
- "This will create an increase in results."
- "You will learn so much at the event."
- "If we start now, we only have to do this much every day."
- "Let's get our first team members now, so they can be learning while we build."
- "If you sponsor three people, you will get this bonus."
- "They will tell you exactly what to do."
- "This is a bit of information overload, so you will be prepared."
- "It will be worth the investment to go to the event."

And now, here is how we will use these phrases.

"You already know this makes sense. So let's get started now."

"This will create an increase in results. Expect a 25% increase in the average order."

"You will learn so much at the event. Bring extra notepads and get ready for the announcements."

"If we start now, we only have to do this much every day. Every day we delay makes our job harder."

"Let's get our first team members now, so they can be learning while we build. We don't want any lag in our growth."

"If you sponsor three people, you will get this bonus. Get your people now before this special bonus ends."

"They will tell you exactly what to do. Just follow the steps."

"This is a bit of information overload, so you will be prepared. You will like it."

"It will be worth the investment to go to the event. Think of the increase in our bonus checks from all the new things we will learn."

Notice that green personalities make prudent, informed choices on the best mode of action. For them, it is a matter of efficiency and effectiveness. It is not about excitement, hype, and enthusiasm.

Phrases for closing.

Getting the green personalities to take action is tough. They want to check, double-check, and then review the information and facts one more time.

Pushing won't work. That will stress them into believing that they are making a decision too fast. Instead, we will use their language combined with facts, and then ask them to make a decision. Here are some examples.

- "Let's start the tax deductions today."
- "It just makes sense to join right away."
- "They did the research. This just makes sense."
- "Let's get a head start on our business."
- "Obviously you want to save money on your taxes."
- "There is no way to fail with the savings."
- "It is the logical choice to join and leverage your time."

Here are some examples of using these phrases.

"Let's start the tax deductions today. Every day we wait we lose more and more of these valuable tax deductions."

"It just makes sense to join right away. We could get the business into momentum before the holidays."

"They did the research, so this just makes sense. We should be happy we don't have to do all that extra researching on our own."

"Let's get a head start on our business. Let's order the big pack and use the extra savings for advertising."

"Obviously you want to save money on your taxes. This makes sense."

"There is no way to fail with the savings. It would be bad not to take the savings."

"It is the logical choice to join and leverage your time. This is more efficient."

What should we do if our green personalities continue to put off making a decision? We need to have empathy. There are obviously some unanswered questions. Let's bring out these questions.

We will ask them, "What would you like to know next?"

We will answer the question as efficiently as possible. Then immediately ask again, "What would you like to know next?"

We will continue this process until they feel all of their questions have been answered. Now, the green personalities will feel more comfortable making their final decision.

Phrases for upselling.

If our business offers optional starter packs, the green personalities normally take the largest pack. Why? Because it will have the best value and the best return on investment. All we need to do is take the time to explain the different options, and what is included.

Our green personality prospects will love all of these details. We then help them make the best decision for their business. Here are some example phrases that green personalities would appreciate.

- "This pack gives you pretty good value."

- "This pack gives you the most leverage with your money."

- "You will save more with the big pack."

- "This is the best value for your money."

- "You can be profitable more quickly with this pack."

- "For a bigger tax deduction, you will want this one."

- "This one just makes sense."

Let's put these phrases into action.

"This pack gives you pretty good value, but not the best value."

"This pack will leverage your money the most, and get the biggest discount."

"You will save more money with the big pack. Then you can use those savings to get even more products."

"This is the best value for your money. We want to make sure our money goes as far as possible."

"You can be profitable more quickly with this pack. It is a big discount from the regular prices."

"For a bigger tax deduction, you will want this one. This is a wise start."

"This one just makes sense. It is the best value."

Speed matters.

At what speed should we talk to green personalities? That should be obvious by now. Slow and deliberate.

Green personalities are indirect. If we ask them a question, we can expect a pause before the answer. Why? First, because they are thinking, "Do I understand the question clearly?" Green personalities place a premium on clear conversation. Second, green personalities want to think about their answer. They want to make sure their answer is clear, and above all, correct. This might take some time.

During this pause, we might feel the need to rush in and fill this gap with conversation. Bad idea. Interrupting the green personalities' thinking with new information is a bad plan. Let's give them a chance to ponder our question and formulate an answer they are comfortable with.

So our conversation with green personalities should be slow and logical. Rushing and talking too fast is counterproductive. This would create skepticism and resistance. Green personalities are already skeptical. We don't want to enhance that.

Green personalities live for data and information. They love it.

Why do green personalities have so many objections?

The fear of the unknown. The crack in the dam. They want to know everything before proceeding forward.

Which magic words will help put our green personality prospects at ease?

"I completely understand."

Our green personality prospects think, "Oh, you are listening to me. And you understand. You must have researched this previously. I feel better already."

Here are some examples of using this phrase to answer objections.

Objection: "I don't want to start yet. Let me wait until I can answer prospects' questions and objections."

Us: "I completely understand why you don't want to start now. You want to be an expert in all areas of our business. However, let's sponsor a few people now, so they can be learning all about our business at the same time."

Objection: "I wish there were more tablets per bottle."

Us: "I completely understand why you wish the tablet count was higher per bottle. It makes sense. Let's submit that suggestion to the home office. Meanwhile, let's continue to build while they investigate the pros and cons of your suggestion."

Objection: "I don't think I know enough at this stage to get started successfully. I would waste my money."

Us: "I completely understand. Nobody wants risk. What if we made a detailed game plan on how to get your first check?"

Objection: "I am not a salesperson. I don't want to be a pushy salesperson."

Us: "I completely understand. Nobody wants to be a sleazy salesperson. Would you like to know a logical game plan so we don't have to be one of those pushy salespeople?"

Objection: "I don't know what to say."

Us: "I completely understand. Would you like to learn how to get others to do all the talking?"

Objection: "I am shy. I don't feel comfortable talking to people."

Us: "I completely understand. Would you like to know how to help people without putting pressure on yourself?"

So what should we do if we get tired of saying "I completely understand" to our prospects?

Instead, we could say, "That makes sense."

Pretty easy. Green personalities love the phrase, "That makes sense." This creates immediate rapport, and allows the green personalities to listen to us without prejudice.

Green personalities have lots of objections. However, they are not trying to resist our sales presentation. Instead, they are trying to make sure they don't overlook something and make a mistake. If we are reasonable, green personalities will welcome the discussion of their objections. They want to solve their uncertainties and questions about our products or services.

Phrases to avoid.

We don't want to make enemies. We can offend green personalities by forcing them to move too fast or get out of their comfort zone. Remember, they want to avoid risk.

Here are some phrases to avoid.

- "You have to do this."
- "Get up and get busy."
- "Just go out and meet a lot of people."
- "Start now. You can learn as you go."

Here are some expanded examples, and what the green personalities think.

"You have to do this our way. Why can't you follow our system?" (Oh, so there are other ways? Let me investigate the other ways first.)

"Get up and get busy. Stop hesitating and make those calls." (I am not ready yet. Stop pushing me. I am a volunteer, not an employee.)

"Just go out and meet a lot of people. What is so hard about that?" (Well, that is hard for me. I don't know how to do that, and I certainly am not comfortable doing it. I am not social.)

"Start now. You can learn as you go. You don't have to have all the answers before you begin." (Yes, I need the answers first. What if someone asks me a question I can't answer?)

Want a deeper understanding of why green personalities do the things they do?

To understand the green personalities better, think of how they prioritize their values. Of the 14 values, many green personalities would have preferences similar to this.

More prominent values:

- Accomplishments.
- Career fulfillment.
- Desire to feel needed.
- Financial security.

Less prominent values:

- Power.
- Desire to look good.
- Loving relationship with partner.
- Family.
- Personal enlightenment.
- Adventure junkie.
- Popularity.
- Desire to have a good time.
- Desire to be rich.
- Aim for fame.

Think about these values. Green personalities don't focus on the latest fashions. Their desire to look good is less prominent. So if our approach is to emphasize how a big bonus check could upgrade their wardrobe, our conversation misses the mark.

People do things based upon their view of the world. Once we know their view, our communication gets better.

Complicated? Challenging?

A bit. Of the four color personalities, the most challenging personality to communicate with is the green personality. They are the least social of the personalities.

So maybe a little humor will help us understand them better. Here is a green personality story.

After 30 years of marriage, the yellow personality wife couldn't take it any longer. She asked that they visit a marriage counselor. The green personality husband reluctantly agreed.

The marriage counselor asked, "So what is the problem?" The yellow personality wife replied, "I need someone to tell me that they love me. I like reassurance every day. But my green personality husband has never once told me that he loves me since we got married."

The marriage counselor turned to the green personality husband and said, "Is this true? Have you never once said that you loved your wife in 30 years of marriage?"

The green personality husband replied, "Yes, it is true. Before we got married, I said that I loved her. And I told her that I would let her know if anything changed."

And that sums up the green personality thinking process.

AND FINALLY ...

No one is going to have a one-color personality. People are more complex than that. However, when we notice someone with extreme personality tendencies, we should make the effort to talk to them using the mini-scripts and phrases we've learned. We can't expect them to adjust to us. We have to make the adjustment. And the reward will be huge. We will see communication and understanding increase before our very eyes.

Over time, this becomes natural. By understanding our prospects' values, we can easily predict which parts of our offering they want to hear.

Will this be fun? Of course.

We can almost make it a game. Let's take cars for example. What kinds of cars would you expect the different color personalities to drive? Let's do a little exaggeration to make it easy to remember.

Yellow personality.

A minivan filled with children, toys, or stuffed animals for the grandchildren.

An electric or hybrid car.

A car full of stickers promoting the environment or some sort of healthy change.

Blue personality.

A fast car painted in a bright neon color.

The car stereo always on full volume.

Every compartment filled with stuff they haven't seen in years.

Red personality.

A luxury car with every option and upgrade installed.

A bright red sports car.

And their car will always be clean, waxed, and bright.

Green personality.

A conservative, practical car with limited upgrades and options.

A fully paid-off car.

Great fuel efficiency with a notebook to log the results.

The "one-size-fits-all" script.

To conclude, sometimes we can't figure out our prospects' color personalities or their values. What can we do? We use a one-size-fits-all script that is easy to remember. So let's finish with the one script we can teach our team in their very first day of business:

"This is the only business where you can make a lot of money, help a bunch of people, and have a ton of fun while doing it. It just makes sense."

THANK YOU.

Thank you for purchasing and reading this book. We hope you found some ideas that will work for you.

Before you go, would it be okay if we asked a small favor? Would you take just one minute and leave a sentence or two reviewing this book online? Your review can help others choose what they will read next. It would be greatly appreciated by many fellow readers.

I travel the world 240+ days each year.
Let me know if you want me to stop in your
area and conduct a live Big Al training.

BigAlSeminars.com

FREE Big Al Training Audios
Magic Words for Prospecting
plus Free eBook and the Big Al Report!

BigAlBooks.com/free

MORE BIG AL BOOKS

Create Influence
10 Ways to Impress and Guide Others

Influence gives us the power to affect others and our world. Get others to take our advice and solutions, and apply them immediately.

Quick Start Guide for Network Marketing
Get Started FAST, Rejection-FREE!

Our new team members are at the peak of their enthusiasm now. Let's give them the fast-start skills to kick-start their business immediately.

The Two-Minute Story for Network Marketing
Create the Big-Picture Story That Sticks!

Worried about presenting your business opportunity to prospects? Here is the solution. The two-minute story is the ultimate presentation to network marketing prospects.

How to Build Your Network Marketing Business in 15 Minutes a Day

Anyone can set aside 15 minutes a day to start building their financial freedom. Of course we would like to have more time, but in just 15 minutes we can change our lives forever.

How to Meet New People Guidebook
Overcome Fear and Connect Now

Meeting new people is easy when we can read their minds. Discover how strangers automatically size us up in seconds, using three basic standards.

Why Are My Goals Not Working?
Color Personalities for Network Marketing Success

Setting goals that work for us is easy when we have guidelines and a checklist.

Closing for Network Marketing
Getting Prospects Across The Finish Line

Here are 46 years' worth of our best closes. All of these closes are kind and comfortable for prospects, and rejection-free for us.

Pre-Closing for Network Marketing
"Yes" Decisions Before The Presentation

Instead of selling to customers with facts, features and benefits, let's talk to prospects in a way they like. We can now get that "yes" decision first, so the rest of our presentation will be easy.

The One-Minute Presentation
Explain Your Network Marketing Business Like A Pro

Learn to make your business grow with this efficient, focused business presentation technique.

Retail Sales for Network Marketers
How to Get New Customers for Your MLM Business

Learn how to position your retail sales so people are happy to buy. Don't know where to find customers for your products and services? Learn how to market to people who want what you offer.

Getting "Yes" Decisions
What insurance agents and financial advisors can say to clients

In the new world of instant decisions, we need to master the words and phrases to successfully move our potential clients to lifelong clients. Easy ... when we can read their minds and service their needs immediately.

3 Easy Habits For Network Marketing
Automate Your MLM Success

Use these habits to create a powerful stream of activity in your network marketing business.

Start SuperNetworking!
5 Simple Steps to Creating Your Own Personal Networking Group

Start your own personal networking group and have new, pre-sold customers and prospects come to you.

The Four Color Personalities for MLM
The Secret Language for Network Marketing

Learn the skill to quickly recognize the four personalities and how to use magic words to translate your message.

Ice Breakers!
How To Get Any Prospect To Beg You For A Presentation

Create unlimited Ice Breakers on-demand. Your distributors will no longer be afraid of prospecting, instead, they will love prospecting.

How To Get Instant Trust, Belief, Influence and Rapport!
13 Ways To Create Open Minds By Talking To The Subconscious Mind

Learn how the pros get instant rapport and cooperation with even the coldest prospects. The #1 skill every new distributor needs.

First Sentences for Network Marketing
How To Quickly Get Prospects On Your Side

Attract more prospects and give more presentations with great first sentences that work.

Motivation. Action. Results.

How Network Marketing Leaders Move Their Teams

Learn the motivational values and triggers our team members have, and learn to use them wisely. By balancing internal motivation and external motivation methods, we can be more effective motivators.

How To Build Network Marketing Leaders

Volume One: Step-By-Step Creation Of MLM Professionals

This book will give you the step-by-step activities to actually create leaders.

How To Build Network Marketing Leaders

Volume Two: Activities And Lessons For MLM Leaders

You will find many ways to change people's viewpoints, to change their beliefs, and to reprogram their actions.

The Complete Three-Book Network Marketing Leadership Series

Series includes: How To Build Network Marketing Leaders Volume One, How To Build Network Marketing Leaders Volume Two, and Motivation. Action. Results.

51 Ways and Places to Sponsor New Distributors

Discover Hot Prospects For Your Network Marketing Business

Learn the best places to find motivated people to build your team and your customer base.

How To Prospect, Sell And Build Your Network Marketing Business With Stories

If you want to communicate effectively, add your stories to deliver your message.

26 Instant Marketing Ideas To Build Your Network Marketing Business

176 pages of amazing marketing lessons and case studies to get more prospects for your business immediately.

Big Al's MLM Sponsoring Magic

How To Build A Network Marketing Team Quickly

This book shows the beginner exactly what to do, exactly what to say, and does it through the eyes of a brand-new distributor.

Public Speaking Magic

Success and Confidence in the First 20 Seconds

By using any of the three major openings in this book, we can confidently start our speeches and presentations without fear.

Worthless Sponsor Jokes

Network Marketing Humor

Here is a collection of worthless sponsor jokes from 25 years of the "Big Al Report." Network marketing can be enjoyable, and we can have fun making jokes along the way.

How To Get Kids To Say Yes!

Using the Secret Four Color Languages to Get Kids to Listen

Turn discipline and frustration into instant cooperation. Kids love to say "yes" when they hear their own color-coded language.

BigAlBooks.com

About the Authors

Keith Schreiter has 20+ years of experience in network marketing and MLM. He shows network marketers how to use simple systems to build a stable and growing business.

So, do you need more prospects? Do you need your prospects to commit instead of stalling? Want to know how to engage and keep your group active? If these are the types of skills you would like to master, you will enjoy his "how-to" style.

Keith speaks and trains in the U.S., Canada, and Europe.

Tom "Big Al" Schreiter has 40+ years of experience in network marketing and MLM. As the author of the original "Big Al" training books in the late '70s, he has continued to speak in over 80 countries on using the exact words and phrases to get prospects to open up their minds and say "YES."

His passion is marketing ideas, marketing campaigns, and how to speak to the subconscious mind in simplified, practical ways. He is always looking for case studies of incredible marketing campaigns that give usable lessons.

As the author of numerous audio trainings, Tom is a favorite speaker at company conventions and regional events.